25 Reproducible Sales Strategies and Activities

Peter R. Garber

HRD Press, Inc. • Amherst • Massachusetts

Published by HRD Press, Inc.
    22 Amherst Road
    Amherst, MA 01002
    800-822-2801 (U.S. and Canada)
    413-253-3488
    413-253-3490 (fax)
    www.hrdpress.com

ISBN 978-1-61014-386-8

Composition by Anctil Virtual Office
Edited by Sally M. Farnham
Cover design by Eileen Klockars

Table of Contents

Introduction

	+				
Relationship	1. Know the Customer	6. What's in a Name?	11. Understand the Customer's Needs	16. Creating Buying Habits	21. Teamwork
	2. Build Rapport	7. Selling Up, Down, All Around	12. Empowering Customers	17. Selling Service	22. Adapting to Change
	3. Honesty is the Best Policy	8. Contingency Selling	13. Cutting Costs	18. Full-Service Selling	23. Beating the Competition
	4. Understand the Customer's Perspective	9. Creating the Need	14. Just-in-Time Opportunities	19. Global Approach	24. Creative Selling
	5. Selling the "Sizzle"	10. Having the Latest Technology	15. Pull-Through Sales	20. Value-Added Sales	25. Worth the Price

– **Performance** +

Welcome to *25 Sales Strategies and Activities*. This is a unique training and development tool. It allows you to not only identify what might be the most appropriate sales strategies to use with your customers, but also provides you help in implementing each one. *25 Sales Strategies and Activities* is not intended to be a one-time training program, but rather an extremely useful and practical ongoing reference guide and resource. It provides a diagnostic Sales Strategy Matrix that can be used in many different ways. The matrix is designed to present each of the 25 sales strategies in relation to two critical factors concerning selling to customers—*relationships* and *performance*.

As you can see on this matrix, the position of each strategy shows how much it emphasizes both relationship and performance. As shown on the vertical axis of the matrix, the relationship index is measured from highest at the top to lowest at the bottom. Relationships deal with how the customer perceives you as a supplier based on past experience and interactions with you. Relationships are always complex and multi-dimensional. Similarly, the performance index is shown on the horizontal axis as highest to the right and lowest to the left. Performance for this purpose is more focused on what you as a supplier actually deliver to the customer. Performance is "where the rubber meets the road" for the customer.

Strategies on the matrix are further classified as highest, higher, moderate, lower, lowest. These measures of relationship and performance for each position on the **Relationship Performance Index** are shown on the next page.

Relationship Performance Index

1. Relationship—highest Performance—lowest	**6.** Relationship—highest Performance—lower	**11.** Relationship—highest Performance—moderate	**16.** Relationship—highest Performance—higher	**21.** Relationship—highest Performance—highest
2. Relationship—higher Performance—lowest	**7.** Relationship—higher Performance—lower	**12.** Relationship—higher Performance—moderate	**17.** Relationship—higher Performance—higher	**22.** Relationship—higher Performance—highest
3. Relationship—moderate Performance—lowest	**8.** Relationship—moderate Performance—lower	**13.** Relationship—moderate Performance—moderate	**18.** Relationship—moderate Performance—higher	**23.** Relationship—moderate Performance—highest
4. Relationship—lower Performance—lowest	**9.** Relationship—lower Performance—lower	**14.** Relationship—lower Performance—moderate	**19.** Relationship—lower Performance—higher	**24.** Relationship—lower Performance—highest
5. Relationship—lowest Performance—lowest	**10.** Relationship—lowest Performance—lower	**15.** Relationship—lowest Performance—moderate	**20.** Relationship—lowest Performance—higher	**25.** Relationship—lowest Performance—highest

To illustrate, look at Know the Customer Strategy, which is positioned in the number 1 block on the matrix in the upper left hand corner. This position on the matrix indicates that this sales strategy would focus highest on the relationship with the customer and lowest on performance. On the opposite extreme on the matrix, you see Worth the Price, the number 25 block in the bottom right hand corner. This position has a lowest measure on relationship and a highest measure on performance. Teamwork in block 21 is highest in both its focus on relationship and performance.

It is important to understand that regardless of where on this matrix a particular strategy may be positioned as either high or low in relationship or performance, both factors are always still important. You cannot have one of these factors at the expense of the other; it is more a matter of focus. Different strategies simply rely more heavily on one or the other of these factors. You need to determine what is best and most appropriate for your particular circumstance. The 25 sales strategies can help you evaluate the situation and make these critical decisions concerning what approach to take with the customer.

Supporting each of the sales strategies are activities specifically designed to help participants implement the selected approach. Many of these activities will help participants develop specific sales strategies for their customers. The activities are presented in an easy-to-use format that clearly explains the objective of each strategy and how it can be implemented. Each activity begins by identifying the focus of the strategy in relation to the relationship and performance indexes. Each activity includes exhibits that have been specific-ally designed to assist you in presenting the concepts and learning objectives of the sales strategy. These exhibits are fully reproducible and can be used as exercises and handouts for each activity.

Not every strategy may be right for your circumstance or with every customer. What is most important is that you have a clear understanding of the possible sales strategies that could be used and the potential strengths and benefits of each one. By thinking in terms of relationships and performance, you can be better able to accurately diagnose what would be the most effective sales strategy to use. The most important skill that a salesperson can develop today is the ability to comfortably use as many of these strategies as possible. The more strategies you can use, the more "tools" you have to increase sales. Think of each of these 25 strategies as a new opportunity to make a sale.

Good luck with your new 25 sales strategies and with your new customers that they will help you find.

Strategy #1

Know the Customer

+					
	1. **Know the Customer**	6. What's in a Name?	11. Understand the Customer's Needs	16. Creating Buying Habits	21. Teamwork
Relationship	2. Build Rapport	7. Selling Up, Down, All Around	12. Empowering Customers	17. Selling Service	22. Adapting to Change
	3. Honesty is the Best Policy	8. Contingency Selling	13. Cutting Costs	18. Full-Service Selling	23. Beating the Competition
	4. Understand the Customer's Perspective	9. Creating the Need	14. Just-in-Time Opportunities	19. Global Approach	24. Creative Selling
⏐	5. Selling the "Sizzle"	10. Having the Latest Technology	15. Pull-Through Sales	20. Value-Added Sales	25. Worth the Price

−   **Performance**   +

Sales Strategy

Relationship—Highest
Performance—Lowest

This strategy is almost entirely focused on building on your relationship with the customer. Knowing the customer is important to virtually every one of the other 24 strategies. It can also be critical to determining which other sales strategies you might want to develop with your customers. Selecting Know the Customer does not diminish your need to perform to the customer's expectations, but rather helps you set the stage for understanding how to accomplish that objective.

Activity

Think of this strategy as if it were a research project. Your objective is to learn as much about the subject as possible. To achieve this, you would seek any number of sources of information. This activity is designed to help you identify where you could find this information that can help you better understand and learn more about your customer(s).

Time

40 minutes

Resources

Exhibits 1-A, 1-B, and 1-C; Customers' annual report, sales literature, advertisements, news services, Internet, or other sources of information about your customers.

Presentation

Review where Know the Customer fits into the Sales Strategy Matrix and why it is positioned where it is. Point out that Know the Customer is in the highest position concerning relationship with the customer. Also, you should make the point that just because this strategy is in the lowest performance area of the matrix, this doesn't mean that it is not important to the customer.

Using Exhibit 1-A, instruct participants to begin developing how they can learn more about their customers. Encourage participants to think of as many different sources of information as they can.

Once participants have completed Exhibit 1-A, introduce the next exhibit. In Exhibit 1-B, participants are now asked how they can use this information to develop more effective sales plans and strategies with their customers. To help participants complete this part of the activity, present Exhibit 1-C, which includes a number of ways that learning more about customers can help them develop more effective sales strategies.

Exhibit 1-A
Potential Sources of Information About Your Customers

_____

_____

_____

_____

_____

_____

_____

_____

_____

_____

_____

_____

_____

_____

Exhibit 1-B
Using Information
About Your Customer

How can you use these sources of information (listed in Exhibit 1-A) to not only get to know your customers better but also develop more effective sales strategies?

_____

_____

_____

_____

_____

_____

_____

_____

_____

_____

_____

_____

_____

_____

Exhibit 1-C
Potential Benefits of
Knowing the Customer

- Gain better understanding of customer's needs and requirements

- Learn more about the customer's business and ways your product/service can be utilized

- Understand your customer's goals and plans for the future and how you can be part of them

- Be better able to suggest ways to improve your customer's business

- Lets the customer know that you are really interested in learning more about them and doing business together

Strategy #2

Build Rapport

+					
	1. Know the Customer	6. What's in a Name?	11. Understand the Customer's Needs	16. Creating Buying Habits	21. Teamwork
	2. Build Rapport	7. Selling Up, Down, All Around	12. Empowering Customers	17. Selling Service	22. Adapting to Change
	3. Honesty is the Best Policy	8. Contingency Selling	13. Cutting Costs	18. Full-Service Selling	23. Beating the Competition
	4. Understand the Customer's Perspective	9. Creating the Need	14. Just-in-Time Opportunities	19. Global Approach	24. Creative Selling
	5. Selling the "Sizzle"	10. Having the Latest Technology	15. Pull-Through Sales	20. Value-Added Sales	25. Worth the Price

Relationship (vertical axis, + top, – bottom)

Performance (horizontal axis, – left, + right)

Sales Strategy

Relationship—Higher
Performance—Lowest

This strategy could easily occupy the highest position on the matrix concerning relationship. It only appears in the number 2 position because of the need to first understand the customer in order to build this rapport. Too often, the importance of building rapport with the customer is either not fully appreciated or worse yet, overlooked. The fact is that your rapport with a customer can be the most important factor in their buying decision-making process. Without this rapport with the customer, there is far less chance of understanding each other's needs and how these can be met through your business relationship together.

Activity

This activity is designed to help participants plan how to build better rapport with their customers. The exhibits are useful because they help participants develop plans for building better rapport with a specific customer. Typically, building rapport is not something that is planned. Rather it is something that just is expected to happen. Unfortunately, rapport does not always spontaneously occur naturally. Rapport can require planning and effort to be utilized in a productive manner as this activity is designed to do.

Time

30 minutes

Resources

Exhibits 2-A and 2-B

Presentation

Review where Build Rapport fits into the Sales Strategy Matrix and why it is positioned where it is.

Present and review Exhibit 2-A, What is Rapport with the Customer? Ask participants what they would add to this description of rapport and how important it is to their business relationship with their customers.

Have participants complete Exhibit 2-B, Rapport Builders, in which they are asked to identify common areas of interest and shared goals that can help them establish better rapport with their customers.

Exhibit 2-A
What is Rapport with the Customer?

Building customer rapport involves learning to communicate with your customer in such a way that is comfortable for each of you. Rapport is established by finding or identifying common goals and interests between you and the customer. Building rapport is essential to establishing a good working relationship with the customer. Rapport with the customer helps establish the trust necessary for this relationship to be mutually beneficial to both of you.

Exhibit 2-B
Rapport Builders

Rapport is created by finding common interest and goals between you and the customer.

A. Think of a customer (or potential one) with whom you would like to build a better rapport. What are some common areas of interest between you and this customer that could help you build a better rapport?

_____

_____

_____

_____

B. What are some common goals that you share together that could help build this rapport with the customer?

_____

_____

_____

_____

C. How can you use both these common areas of interest and goals to build rapport with your customer?

_____

_____

_____

_____

Strategy #3

Honesty is the Best Policy

+					
	1. Know the Customer	6. What's in a Name?	11. Understand the Customer's Needs	16. Creating Buying Habits	21. Teamwork
	2. Build Rapport	7. Selling Up, Down, All Around	12. Empowering Customers	17. Selling Service	22. Adapting to Change
	3. Honesty is the Best Policy	8. Contingency Selling	13. Cutting Costs	18. Full-Service Selling	23. Beating the Competition
	4. Understand the Customer's Perspective	9. Creating the Need	14. Just-in-Time Opportunities	19. Global Approach	24. Creative Selling
	5. Selling the "Sizzle"	10. Having the Latest Technology	15. Pull-Through Sales	20. Value-Added Sales	25. Worth the Price

Relationship (vertical axis, + top, – bottom)

−   **Performance**   +

Sales Strategy

Relationship—Moderate
Performance—Lowest

Honesty is the Best Policy is really less of a sales strategy as it is a guiding principle for dealing with your customers. It is not optional as might be many of the other strategies presented. It appears where it does on the matrix because it forms the core or center for your relationship with the customer. It is not directly linked to performance, but certainly has an influence. This influence may be more related to how the customer ultimately perceives performance. For example, if the customer thinks that he/she is not being dealt with honestly, everything concerning the sale, including the quality of the product or service, will come into question.

Activity

The activity emphasizes the importance of selling with honesty and integrity. It demonstrates the consequences of selling these principles and the longer-term problems this can create.

Time

30 minutes

Resources

Exhibits 3-A and 3-B

Presentation

Review where Honesty is the Best Policy fits into the Sales Strategy Matrix and why it is positioned where it is.

Present Exhibit 3-A, and read the quote to participants. Ask participants what they believe this means to them and their business relationships with their customers.

Ask participants to think about circumstances that they may be aware of in which this principle wasn't followed. Note: Be careful not to ask participants to disclose any possible circumstances when they may have been less than honest with a customer in order to make a sale. However, if this information is volunteered, it may be acceptable to develop this dialog. As an alternative, you could ask participants to share experiences as customers themselves when they felt they were deceived about the product or service they purchased. Discuss how this affected their business relationship and if they continued doing business with that supplier in the future.

Using Exhibit 3-B, Customer Reality Check, have participants complete the columns in this exercise. Discuss where they may have discovered that their customers might be unintentionally getting the wrong impression or perception about their product or service and how this misunderstanding could and should be corrected. Emphasize that the objective of this activity is not to imply that anyone is intentionally being dishonest with a customer, but rather to emphasize the importance of building a working relationship with the customer based on honesty. Exhibit 3-B is designed to help ensure that there are no misunderstandings from the customer's perspective and that they perceive participants as being completely open and honest with them.

Exhibit 3-A

Honesty isn't just the best policy;
it is the *only* policy when dealing with the customer.

Exhibit 3-B
Customer Reality Check

A. How might your customer's perceptions about your product/ service be incorrect or unrealistic?	B. What customer perceptions might need to be clarified or corrected?	C. What would be the short-term consequences of clarifying or correcting these misperceptions?	D. What might be the long-term consequences of clarifying or correcting these misperceptions?

Strategy #4

Understand the Customer's Perspective

+					
	1. Know the Customer	6. What's in a Name?	11. Understand the Customer's Needs	16. Creating Buying Habits	21. Teamwork
	2. Build Rapport	7. Selling Up, Down, All Around	12. Empowering Customers	17. Selling Service	22. Adapting to Change
Relationship	3. Honesty is the Best Policy	8. Contingency Selling	13. Cutting Costs	18. Full-Service Selling	23. Beating the Competition
	4. Understand the Customer's Perspective	9. Creating the Need	14. Just-in-Time Opportunities	19. Global Approach	24. Creative Selling
–	5. Selling the "Sizzle"	10. Having the Latest Technology	15. Pull-Through Sales	20. Value-Added Sales	25. Worth the Price

–   **Performance**   **+**

Sales Strategy

Relationship—lower
Performance—lowest

Although this strategy does appear in a lower position on the relationship continuum, it still strongly impacts how effectively you are able to deal with the customer. However, this strategy works more "behind the scenes" than directly with the customer. It is more of an introspective look at how you are meeting the customer's requirements than many of the higher relationship strategies on the matrix. Understanding the customer's perspective helps you be better prepared to both build a stronger relationship as well as improve your performance as perceived by the customer. Sometimes we think we are doing what is expected when in reality the customer's perspective is something very different. By better understanding the customer's perspective, you can save both the customer and yourself a great deal of time and frustration by addressing that which is most important.

Activity

You might have seen one of those pictures that can be perceived in more than one way. For instance, you might look at the picture and see an old woman and look at it again and see a young woman. It all depends on your perspective. Similarly, both you and the customer may have different perspectives as well. The customer might feel that certain requirements concerning the service or product you provide are more critical or important than you perceive them to be. Under this circumstance, unless you can gain a better understanding of the customer's perspective, you will continue to fall short of the customer's expectations. This activity is designed to help you gain this better understanding from the customer's perception of what they perceive to be most important concerning the product or service you provide to them. In this activity, you will be asked to compare and possibly contrast how the customer perceives you to your own perceptions.

Time

40 minutes

Resources

Exhibits 4-A and 4-B

Presentation

Review where Understand the Customer's Perspective fits into the Sales Strategy Matrix and why it is positioned where it is.

Begin the activity by emphasizing how important it is to understand the customer's perspective and how this can ultimately affect their buying decisions in the future. Perceptions are reality to the customer. It matters far less how you perceive something than how the customer does.

Ask participants to answer the questions in Exhibit 4-A for themselves as they think the customer would from his/her perspective.

Suggest that participants ask these same three questions (Exhibit 4-B) of their customer(s). Participants can then compare their perceptions to those of the customer. If there are any "surprises" concerning the customer's perceptions relating their expectations and requirements, participants should take the appropriate actions to address these issues.

Conclude the activity by again reminding participants that it is the customer's perspective that is most important. It is these perceptions that will ultimately determine if they will continue to do business with you or not. You need to continuously keep in touch with the customer's perceptions to ensure that you are still meeting their requirements and expectations.

Exhibit 4-A
Customer's Perceptions—Part 1

Instructions: *Answer for yourself* what you think will be your customer's perceptions concerning the following questions.

1. From the customer's perception, what do you believe they would consider to be their most important requirement concerning buying your product or service?

2. How are you presently meeting the customer's requirements concerning this aspect of your business relationship?

3. How could you improve your performance concerning this requirement?

Exhibit 4-B
Customer's Perceptions—Part 2

In order to help better understand how I/we can meet your requirements as a customer, please answer the following questions.

1. From your perception, what do you believe is the most important requirement concerning buying my/our product or service?

_____

_____

_____

_____

_____

2. How well am I/we presently meeting your requirements concerning this aspect of our business relationship?

_____

_____

_____

_____

3. How could I/we improve my/our performance concerning this requirement?

_____

_____

_____

_____

Strategy #5

Selling the "Sizzle"

+				
1. Know the Customer	6. What's in a Name?	11. Understand the Customer's Needs	16. Creating Buying Habits	21. Teamwork
2. Build Rapport	7. Selling Up, Down, All Around	12. Empowering Customers	17. Selling Service	22. Adapting to Change
3. Honesty is the Best Policy	8. Contingency Selling	13. Cutting Costs	18. Full-Service Selling	23. Beating the Competition
4. Understand the Customer's Perspective	9. Creating the Need	14. Just-in-Time Opportunities	19. Global Approach	24. Creative Selling
5. **Selling the "Sizzle"**	10. Having the Latest Technology	15. Pull-Through Sales	20. Value-Added Sales	25. Worth the Price

Relationship (vertical axis, + to –)

Performance (horizontal axis, – to +)

Sales Strategy

Relationship—lowest
Performance—lowest

You might wonder why you would ever use a sales strategy that was low in both relationship and performance. After all—what's left? However, there are times when this might be the most effective strategy to use. Obviously, you wouldn't use this strategy in a circumstance in which either relationship or performance would be a critical or determining factor for the customer. The type of situation in which you could use this strategy might be when these factors are less important to making the sale (for instance, when you might be selling the same or very similar product or service as your competition; thus performance would be the same for the customer regardless of who they buy from). The customer relationship factor could also be neutralized by lack of any real opportunity to add value to it. You might simply have no opportunity to do anything more than provide the product/service to the customer. In these circumstances, it might be the "sizzle" not the "steak" that gains you customers. This is particularly true if all your competitors are selling the same "steak" as you. Yours just may happen to have more "sizzle" when it cooks than your competitors'. Listen, you can almost hear that sizzle now!

Activity

This activity involves helping participants learn to identify what might be considered "sizzle" in their product or service and how to sell this to the customer.

Time

20 minutes

Resources

Exhibit 5-A

Presentation

Review where Selling the "Sizzle" fits into the Sales Strategy Matrix and why it is positioned where it is.

Discuss why it is still very important, even though it occupies the lowest spot on the matrix on both relationship and performance. Review those circumstances when this strategy might be most effective.

Present Exhibit 5-A and read the quote to participants, which expands the concept on which this activity is based: "It is not the steak that sells, but its sizzle." This means that often it is not the product or service itself that is attractive to the customer, but a benefit or feature of it. This may be what differentiates the product/ service from all the rest that are available to customers on the market. This is a very important fundamental concept in much of the advertising we see everyday. For example, it is not the automobile itself that is the focus of the advertiser's selling strategy, but rather the envy, or prestige, or safety, or comfort, or some other "sizzle" that is being promoted.

Ask participants what the "sizzle" might be for their product or service and discuss how and when they might better use this as a selling strategy.

Exhibit 5-A

"It is not the steak that sells, but its sizzle."

Strategy #6

What's in a Name?

+					
Relationship	1. Know the Customer	6. **What's in a Name?**	11. Understand the Customer's Needs	16. Creating Buying Habits	21. Teamwork
	2. Build Rapport	7. Selling Up, Down, All Around	12. Empowering Customers	17. Selling Service	22. Adapting to Change
	3. Honesty is the Best Policy	8. Contingency Selling	13. Cutting Costs	18. Full-Service Selling	23. Beating the Competition
	4. Understand the Customer's Perspective	9. Creating the Need	14. Just-in-Time Opportunities	19. Global Approach	24. Creative Selling
–	5. Selling the "Sizzle"	10. Having the Latest Technology	15. Pull-Through Sales	20. Value-Added Sales	25. Worth the Price

–   Performance   +

Sales Strategy

Relationship—highest
Performance—lower

This strategy is focused on building your relationship with the customer, but begins to move more toward performance. It is about the importance of names in business. Unfortunately, most of the time, names are thought of as necessary, but not strategic. Names can open doors for you that would otherwise remain closed. Part of your business goals should be to learn as many of your customers' organizations' names as possible, or at least know where to access this important information. Names of products, processes, policies, materials, principles, etc., that are important to your customer should also be of great interest to you.

Activity

You could call this one "The Name Game." It asks participants to think about how important names are in their dealing with customers. The activity makes the analogy of a name as being like a key. These "keys" can unlock doors in the customer's organization that would otherwise not have been accessible to you. However, forgetting or misplacing a name of a customer can be losing your keys. Without your keys, you cannot do even the most basic of life's functions such as operate your car or enter your home. Names, like keys, are important to give us access to where we want to go.

Time

40 minutes

Resources

Exhibits 6-A and 6-B; possibly the customer's directory of personnel, reporting charts, or other information about each participant's customers' organizations.

Presentation

Explain where What's in a Name? fits into the Sales Strategy Matrix and why it is positioned where it is.

Ask participants to think of the names of their customers as if they were keys that open doors that lead to increased sales.

To further create this analogy, suggest that forgetting a customer's name or not having it available is like losing the keys to your car: Without it, you just can't go where you want to go.

Using Exhibit 6-A, ask participants to identify the names of customers who are the keys to their success.

Conclude the activity with a discussion related to the concept that it is not only the names of people in the customer's organization that are important. The names of products, processes, services, locations, technologies, etc., are also key to effectively dealing with customers. Use Exhibit 6-B to help participants list the other "keys."

Exhibit 6-A

What are some of the most important names of your customers who are the "keys" to the success of your working relationship?

_____

_____

_____

_____

_____

Exhibit 6-B
Other Key Names

What are names (other than those of people) that are important in your interactions with customers? They might include names of products, processes, services, locations, technologies, etc., that are important to know when dealing with customers?

_____

_____

_____

_____

How can you learn more about these key names as they relate to your customers?

_____

_____

_____

_____

What might be some additional sources to learn more names of key people in your customer's organization?

_____

_____

_____

_____

Strategy #7

Selling Up, Down, All Around

+					
	1. Know the Customer	6. What's in a Name?	11. Understand the Customer's Needs	16. Creating Buying Habits	21. Teamwork
	2. Build Rapport	7. **Selling Up, Down, All Around**	12. Empowering Customers	17. Selling Service	22. Adapting to Change
	3. Honesty is the Best Policy	8. Contingency Selling	13. Cutting Costs	18. Full-Service Selling	23. Beating the Competition
	4. Understand the Customer's Perspective	9. Creating the Need	14. Just-in-Time Opportunities	19. Global Approach	24. Creative Selling
	5. Selling the "Sizzle"	10. Having the Latest Technology	15. Pull-Through Sales	20. Value-Added Sales	25. Worth the Price

Relationship (vertical axis, + top, – bottom)

– Performance +

Sales Strategy

Relationship—higher
Performance—lower

This strategy is based on the belief that often it is as important *who* you know as it is *what* you know. Often, regardless of how good a service or product is that you have to offer, if you don't make your sales presentation to the right people, you won't get the business. You need to get the attention of people on many levels of the customer's organization before a buying decision can be made.

Activity

This activity focuses on developing strategies concerning who you have contact with in the customer's organization. It asks participants to think about and identify who makes the buying decisions in their customer's organization and about developing strategies to influence these decisions.

Time

40 minutes

Resources

Exhibits 7-A and 7-B; information on customer's organization including reporting charts if available

Presentation

Review where Selling Up, Down, and All Around fits into the Sales Strategy Matrix and why it is positioned where it is.

Present Exhibit 7-A, Who Makes the Buying Decision in Your Customer's Organization? and have participants fill in the blanks concerning this question.

Lead a discussion about the importance of identifying who the customer's decision makers are as well as who influences buying decisions. Have participants identify these individuals on Exhibit 7-A.

Next show Exhibit 7-B, Who Really is the Customer? and lead a discussion on the concept of purchaser and consumer. Discuss who really is the customer in this scenario, the dog or the dog owner as described in the exhibit. You might ask this same question in relation to children's breakfast cereal—"If a child doesn't like the taste of the cereal, will the parent continue to buy it?" Ask participants how this concept of purchaser and consumer might relate to their business.

To summarize this activity, ask the following question: "Of all the people (or animals!) that have been identified in this activity—decision makers, influencers, purchasers, and customers—who is the most important to your success in making the sale? The correct answer should be that each of them is critically important in the customer's overall buying process and that each of their needs and interests must be understood and addressed.

Exhibit 7-A
Who Makes the Buying Decision in Your Customer's Organization?

Just who really makes the buying decision in your customer's organization might not always be clear or easily identified. In other words, who are the decision makers? These decision makers might actually be at all levels of the organization and might include people you don't have direct contact with. In this circumstance, the person you deal directly with may be an influencer in the buying decision-making process. Influencers are still extremely important and may have a significant impact on the final buying decision of the decision makers.

Identify who is involved in the buying decision-making process in your customer's organization by filling in the blanks below. Then identify the role of each of these people in the customer's decision-making process by circling either Decision Maker or Influencer.

⇓

Name: _____

Decision Maker or
Influencer?

⇒

Name: _____

Decision Maker or
Influencer?

**Buying
Decision**

⇐

Name: _____

Decision Maker or
Influencer?

Name: _____

Decision Maker or
Influencer?

⇑

Exhibit 7-B
Who Really is the Customer?

**If the dog doesn't like the taste of the dog food,
will the owner continue to buy it?**

In this case, who really is the customer—the dog or its owner?

Strategy #8

Contingency Selling

+					
	1. Know the Customer	6. What's in a Name?	11. Understand the Customer's Needs	16. Creating Buying Habits	21. Teamwork
	2. Build Rapport	7. Selling Up, Down, All Around	12. Empowering Customers	17. Selling Service	22. Adapting to Change
	3. Honesty is the Best Policy	**8. Contingency Selling**	13. Cutting Costs	18. Full-Service Selling	23. Beating the Competition
	4. Understand the Customer's Perspective	9. Creating the Need	14. Just-in-Time Opportunities	19. Global Approach	24. Creative Selling
–	5. Selling the "Sizzle"	10. Having the Latest Technology	15. Pull-Through Sales	20. Value-Added Sales	25. Worth the Price

Relationship (vertical axis), Performance − + (horizontal axis)

Sales Strategy

Relationship—Moderate
Performance—Lower

Contingency Selling could easily be argued to be higher on the performance scale. However, having contingency plans is also important to your relationship with your customer. Customer's want to be assured that you can be counted on to provide your product or service without interruption for as long as they want.

Activity

This activity involves developing contingency plans to ensure that the customer feels secure and confident in the participant's ability to continuously provide their product/service without interruption.

Time

30 minutes

Resources

Exhibits 8-A and 8-B

Presentation

Review where Contingency Selling fits into the Sales Strategy Matrix and why it is positioned where it is.

Present Exhibit 8-A and review the definition of *contingency*. Explain why the concept of contingency selling is important to customers—because they need to feel confident in their suppliers' ability to continuously meet their needs and requirements in the event of something unforeseen occurring.

Next present Exhibit 8-B, Planning for the Unexpected. Have participants complete all four parts of the exercise, emphasizing again why this strategy appears higher on the relationship index of the matrix than it does on performance. The main focus of this strategy is to give the customer more confidence in their ability to continuously provide uninterrupted product service, even if the unexpected occurs.

A final discussion point may be, "At what cost should a supplier be willing to ensure this uninterrupted delivery of product or service to the customer?" This ultimately is a question that each participant has to answer for themselves.

Exhibit 8-A

Definition:

---

contingency selling: planning for any possible or unforeseen occurrence to ensure the customer uninterrupted delivery of product or service

---

Exhibit 8-B
Planning for the Unexpected

What might be examples of some of these unexpected events or situations that could occur that would affect your ability to supply your customers?

_____

_____

_____

_____

What could be some things you could plan ahead to do that would prevent these unexpected events from affecting your customers?

_____

_____

_____

_____

What would be the benefit to your customers as a result of these contingency selling plans?

_____

_____

_____

_____

How can you make these plans part of your overall selling strategy with your customers?

_____

_____

_____

Strategy #9

Creating the Need

+					
	1. Know the Customer	6. What's in a Name?	11. Understand the Customer's Needs	16. Creating Buying Habits	21. Teamwork
	2. Build Rapport	7. Selling Up, Down, All Around	12. Empowering Customers	17. Selling Service	22. Adapting to Change
Relationship	3. Honesty is the Best Policy	8. Contingency Selling	13. Cutting Costs	18. Full-Service Selling	23. Beating the Competition
	4. Understand the Customer's Perspective	**9. Creating the Need**	14. Just-in-Time Opportunities	19. Global Approach	24. Creative Selling
–	5. Selling the "Sizzle"	10. Having the Latest Technology	15. Pull-Through Sales	20. Value-Added Sales	25. Worth the Price

–　　　　　　　　　　**Performance**　　　　　　　　　　**+**

Sales Strategy

Relationship—lower
Performance—lower

This strategy is lower on both the relationship and performance indexes because it focuses on something external to both the supplier and the customer. Creating the Need does not mean that you should sell something to the customer that they do not need. Rather, this sales strategy is really more of an education process in which you help customers understand how they can benefit from buying your product or service.

Activity

This activity presents the Fact-Benefit-Result Sales Model. Using this model, participants can learn how to present their product/service in a manner that helps the customer better understand why he/she should make the purchase.

Time

30 minutes

Resources

Exhibits 9-A and 9-B

Presentation

Review where Creating the Need fits into the Sales Strategy Matrix and why it is positioned where it is.

Present Exhibit 9-A, the Fact-Benefit-Result Model. Review the three steps and provide examples of each appropriate for the participants' business situations.

Have participants complete Exhibit 9-B, Using the Fact-Benefit-Result Model, to prepare for a sales presentation to a customer. Make the information in Exhibit 9-A available to participants in a handout to use as a reference tool. Encourage participants to use this model in the future to better explain why the customer needs to buy their product or service.

Summarize this activity by discussing how the Fact-Benefit-Result Model, can help their customers better understand why they would need their product or service. Reinforce once again the concept that creating the need is not intended to mean that you sell something to someone who has no need for the product/service, but rather is an educational process of why they have this need.

Exhibit 9-A
The Fact-Benefit-Result Model

The Fact-Benefit-Result Model is designed to help you present information to the customer to help them understand why they need to use your product or service. For this model to be most effective, you need to use the sequence of Fact-Benefit-Result when presenting to the customer. The model takes much of the emotion out of a customer's buying decision and instead focuses on their needs and how they can be best fulfilled.

The Fact-Benefit-Result Model is easy to use by addressing each of these steps to the customer:

Step 1: Fact. Start by explaining the facts about your product or service to the customer. This might include statistics, comparative data, research, performance studies, experiments, etc., that are available and demonstrate the effectiveness of what you have to sell. An example of a fact might be, "Research has shown our product to be 15 percent more effective than any of our competitors' similarly priced products."

Step 2: Benefit. Next explain the benefits of using your product or service. These benefits should be backed up or supported by the facts previously presented. For example, the benefit of the fact presented in Step 1 above might be, ". . . and this increased efficiency will help you reduce operating costs."

Step 3: Results. Results represent the bottom line of this process. Results are what the customer ultimately hopes to achieve. Results are what justify the expenditure of buying your product or service. Thus it is critically important that you explain exactly what the customer should ultimately expect as a result of buying from you. Following the example presented in Steps 1 and 2, the result would be, "Based on this increased efficiency, the result will be a reduction in your costs that will increase your profitability and ability to meet your customers' requirements."

Desired results are what every business wants to achieve. By explaining in a sequential manner what the process would be to achieve these desired results, you help the customer better understand exactly how this goal can be obtained. This is much more convincing than merely telling the customer what results to expect without any explanation of how or why they are to be accomplished.

Exhibit 9-B
Using the Fact-Benefit-Result Model

Step 1: Facts

_____

_____

_____

_____

Step 2: Benefits

_____

_____

_____

_____

Step 3: Results

_____

_____

_____

_____

Strategy #10

Having the Latest Technology

+					
Relationship	1. Know the Customer	6. What's in a Name?	11. Understand the Customer's Needs	16. Creating Buying Habits	21. Teamwork
	2. Build Rapport	7. Selling Up, Down, All Around	12. Empowering Customers	17. Selling Service	22. Adapting to Change
	3. Honesty is the Best Policy	8. Contingency Selling	13. Cutting Costs	18. Full-Service Selling	23. Beating the Competition
	4. Understand the Customer's Perspective	9. Creating the Need	14. Just-in-Time Opportunities	19. Global Approach	24. Creative Selling
−	5. Selling the "Sizzle"	**10. Having the Latest Technology**	15. Pull-Through Sales	20. Value-Added Sales	25. Worth the Price

−　　　　　　　　　　　　**Performance**　　　　　　　　　　　　+

Sales Strategy

Relationship—lowest
Performance—lower

Technology can be a tremendous advantage in sales, and having the latest technology can put you way out in front of your competition. If you find yourself in this fortunate position, then your relationship with the customer, although still important, is not nearly as critical to your success. The technology itself will most likely address the performance aspect of what you have to sell, again giving you a distinct advantage in this area as well.

Activity

This activity is designed to encourage participants to think about both the current technology and future technology that is part of their product or service. This technology may be either a feature of their product/service or could be part of their marketing and selling strategy.

Time

40 minutes

Resources

Exhibits 10-A and 10-B; product or service literature and specifications concerning participants' business

Presentation

Review where Having the Latest Technology fits into the Sales Strategy Matrix and why it is positioned where it is.

Present Exhibit 10-A, What's Your Technological Advantage? and have participants complete and discuss the questions in the activity.

Have participants complete Exhibit 10-B, Technology Impact Analysis. Discuss the concept of direct and indirect impact. Emphasize that both these roles can be very important in the development of technological advances.

A final point to make is that we must ensure that what we think are technological advances are seen the same way by the customer. Explain that regardless how remarkable the technological advance, if it is not useful to the customer, it has little or even no value.

Exhibit 10-A
What's Your
Technological Advantage?

What technology does your organization presently have to offer the customer that you might not be emphasizing enough?

_____

_____

_____

A technological advantage can put you out in front of your competition. What technological advance would give you a distinct advantage over your competition?

_____

_____

_____

_____

What is the likelihood of this technology being developed?

_____

_____

_____

(continued)

Exhibit 10-A
What's Your
Technological Advantage?
(concluded)

If not soon, when do you think this technology will be available?

_____

How would this technology change the way you do business?

_____

_____

_____

_____

_____

_____

Exhibit 10-B
Technology Impact Analysis

How can you influence or impact the development of technology?

To help you understand this question, answer the following questions.

1. Are you in a position to have an impact on developing this technology, either directly or indirectly? How and why?

_____

_____

_____

_____

2. If directly, how can you help this development be accomplished and made available soon to your organization?

_____

_____

_____

_____

_____

_____

_____

(continued)

Exhibit 10-B
Technology Impact Analysis
(concluded)

3. If indirectly, how can you help ensure that those who are directly responsible for this development are aware of the need for and importance of this technology?

_____

_____

_____

_____

_____

_____

_____

_____

_____

Strategy #11

Understand the Customer's Needs

+	1. Know the Customer	6. What's in a Name?	11. **Understand the Customer's Needs**	16. Creating Buying Habits	21. Teamwork
	2. Build Rapport	7. Selling Up, Down, All Around	12. Empowering Customers	17. Selling Service	22. Adapting to Change
	3. Honesty is the Best Policy	8. Contingency Selling	13. Cutting Costs	18. Full-Service Selling	23. Beating the Competition
	4. Understand the Customer's Perspective	9. Creating the Need	14. Just-in-Time Opportunities	19. Global Approach	24. Creative Selling
	5. Selling the "Sizzle"	10. Having the Latest Technology	15. Pull-Through Sales	20. Value-Added Sales	25. Worth the Price

Relationship (vertical axis, + top, − bottom)

−   **Performance**   +

Sales Strategy

Relationship—highest
Performance—moderate

This strategy is focused strongly on relationships that are essential to understanding the customer's needs. Meeting the customer's needs is the true definition of quality. A sales strategy based on this objective needs to be committed to providing the highest quality product or service possible to meet the customer's needs. But first you must understand these needs and how you can achieve this understanding.

Activity

This activity helps participants learn how they can better understand the needs of their customers. An important point emphasized in the activity is that it is the customer who determines these needs—not the salesperson. Even strategies that focus on creating customer needs (see Strategy #9) ultimately lead to the customer making the final decision concerning what is or is not important to them and their business.

Time

30 minutes

Resources

Exhibits 11-A and 11-B; flipchart

Presentation

Review where Understand the Customer's Needs fits into the Sales Strategy Matrix and why it is positioned where it is.

Present Exhibit 11-A and ask participants the question highlighted: "Why is it important to understand your customer's needs?" Have participants answer this question and then ask the group to share their answers. Record their responses on a flipchart.

Emphasize the fact that if the needs of the participants' customers are not truly understood, then they could spend a great deal of time and energy trying to do things for the customer that the customer doesn't really care about. Even worse, despite all this effort, the customer's real needs still are not being met.

Next, present Exhibit 11-B, 25 Ways to Better Understand Your Customer's Needs. Ask participants which of these ways they could use more effectively to better understand their customer's needs.

Ask participants to develop their own strategy for better understanding their customer's needs based on the suggestions found in Exhibit 11-B or any other ideas they might have. List these ideas on a flipchart.

Exhibit 11-A

Why is it important to understand your customer's needs?

Exhibit 11-B
25 Ways to Better Understand Your Customer's Needs

1. Ask them.
2. Study their buying habits.
3. Learn more about their business.
4. Read their annual report.
5. Read their promotional material.
6. Spend time at their facilities or locations.
7. Visit their Web page on the Internet.
8. Study their company's history.
9. Research the markets they serve.
10. Keep good notes when talking to your customers.
11. Send them a customer satisfaction survey.
12. Make courtesy calls to them to make sure their needs are met.
13. Ask for a copy of their company's mission statement.
14. Ask them what type of training you could provide concerning your product/service.
15. Study business trends that directly affect them.
16. Pay attention to what their CEO says and writes about.
17. Thoroughly investigate any problems they might experience with your product/service.
18. Frequently review customer's quality requirements with them.
19. Ensure that customer's specifications are kept updated.
20. Link yourself electronically (e-mail, intranet, Internet, fax, pager) with the customer.
21. Give customer access to you on off-hours (by pager, home phone, e-mail, fax).
22. Keep informed about the customer's industry trends and changes.
23. Attend conferences that relate to your customer's business.
24. Periodically invite the customer to lunch or dinner.
25. *Really* listen to what the customer is saying to you. They are probably telling you how to keep their business!

Strategy #12

Empowering Customers

+					
	1. Know the Customer	6. What's in a Name?	11. Understand the Customer's Needs	16. Creating Buying Habits	21. Teamwork
	2. Build Rapport	7. Selling Up, Down, All Around	**12. Empowering Customers**	17. Selling Service	22. Adapting to Change
Relationship	3. Honesty is the Best Policy	8. Contingency Selling	13. Cutting Costs	18. Full-Service Selling	23. Beating the Competition
	4. Understand the Customer's Perspective	9. Creating the Need	14. Just-in-Time Opportunities	19. Global Approach	24. Creative Selling
–	5. Selling the "Sizzle"	10. Having the Latest Technology	15. Pull-Through Sales	20. Value-Added Sales	25. Worth the Price

–   Performance   +

Sales Strategy

Relationship—higher
Performance—moderate

Empowering customers requires that a solid relationship and performance history be already established with the customer. Empowerment involves trusting others to make important decisions and to take action. Empowering customers enables them to make critical decisions concerning doing business with you. This goes beyond the normal decisions that a customer might make such as the quality, delivery time, reorder point, etc., that would normally be part of their buying process. Empowering the customer puts him or her in control of many of the decisions and actions that you might normally control. This way the customer is not totally dependent on you to get the product or service that you provide. Ultimately, everyone's needs are met in a more effective and efficient manner.

Activity

This activity explores ways in which participants can empower their customers to take a more active role in the buying process. You might need to caution participants on this activity because it may represent concepts or philosophies very different than normally employed when dealing with customers—it may not be for everyone. Some participants might be reluctant to give customers this much control or responsibility in the buying process for fear that their own value or necessity might be diminished. In other words, if you empower your customers to take control of some of the responsibilities that you presently perform, will the customer continue to feel that he/she still needs you? The answer is "yes." The objective of empowering the customer is to streamline the buying process as much as possible and provide you the opportunity to be of service to the customer in even more important and value-added ways. It is not simply "dumping" your work off onto the customer, nor is it an abdication of your responsibilities to the customer in any way.

Time

40 minutes

Resources

Exhibits 12-A, 12-B, and 12-C

Presentation

Review where Empower the Customer fits into the Sales Strategy Matrix and why it is positioned where it is.

Present Exhibit 12-A, Empowering Customers to Buy. Review how the concept of empowerment is defined in this situation and compare this meaning to what participants' perceptions of its meaning might be.

Ask participants how they believe their customers might be empowered to buy from them. Follow up this question by asking how this approach might change the buying habits of their customers.

Review Exhibit 12-B, How to Empower the Customer.

Using Exhibit 12-C, ask participants to think of additional ways to empower their customers and what the benefits would be of each one.

Exhibit 12-A
Empowering Customers to Buy

Empowering the customer involves enabling them to make more decisions and take more actions concerning buying your product or service. It puts much of the *control* of the buying process in the hands of the customer.

Exhibit 12-B
How to Empower the Customer

Everyone wants to be able to be more in control of those factors that are important to them, and your customers are no different. The concept and principles of empowerment involve moving decision making and even problem solving to those who are in the best positions to accept these responsibilities. There are a number of ways to empower your customers as part of their decision-making and purchasing process. The following are just a few of the ways to empower your customers:

- Empower the customer to be able to reorder from you without your involvement.

- Empower customers to contact your suppliers directly.

- Empower customers to be involved in your pricing decisions.

- Empower customers to provide input into marketing decisions for your company.

- Empower customers to resolve problems concerning your product/service by themselves.

- Empower customers to contact different people and resources within your organization directly without having to go through you first.

- Empower customers to give you feedback about the quality of your product or services without you asking for it.

Exhibit 12-C

Other Ways to Empower the Customer	Benefits
_____	_____
_____	_____
_____	_____
_____	_____
_____	_____
_____	_____
_____	_____
_____	_____
_____	_____
_____	_____
_____	_____
_____	_____
_____	_____
_____	_____
_____	_____

Strategy #13

Cutting Costs

+					
	1. Know the Customer	6. What's in a Name?	11. Understand the Customer's Needs	16. Creating Buying Habits	21. Teamwork
	2. Build Rapport	7. Selling Up, Down, All Around	12. Empowering Customers	17. Selling Service	22. Adapting to Change
Relationship	3. Honesty is the Best Policy	8. Contingency Selling	**13. Cutting Costs**	18. Full-Service Selling	23. Beating the Competition
	4. Understand the Customer's Perspective	9. Creating the Need	14. Just-in-Time Opportunities	19. Global Approach	24. Creative Selling
−	5. Selling the "Sizzle"	10. Having the Latest Technology	15. Pull-Through Sales	20. Value-Added Sales	25. Worth the Price

−　　　　　　　　　　**Performance**　　　　　　　　　　**+**

Sales Strategy

Relationship—moderate
Performance—moderate

As you can see, the Cutting Costs strategy is positioned in the very center of the matrix. Costs are so important to the customer that they are neither solely determined by relationship or performance. Costs are seemingly in a category all its own.

Activity

This activity explores how important costs are to the customer. The Customer Cost Calculator activity helps participants gain a better understanding of how to judge the relative importance of costs to their customers.

Time

30 minutes

Resources

Exhibit 13-A

Presentation

Review where Cutting Costs fits into the Sales Strategy Matrix and why it is positioned where it is.

Begin the activity by discussing how important costs are to customers. Ask participants specifically how important costs are to their customers.

Introduce Exhibit 13-A, Customer Cost Calculator, and have participants complete the questions.

Review scoring and have each participant calculate his/her customer's cost profile based on the interpretations of each scoring range.

Exhibit 13-A
Customer Cost Calculator

Answer the following questions concerning costs and your customer(s):

A. If you raised the price of your product or service, how likely would it be that your customer would look for another supplier?

1 Not Likely	**2**	**3** Fairly Likely	**4**	**5** Highly Likely

B. If you demonstrated to your customer that you needed to raise your price to maintain the quality of your product or service would they most likely:

1 Understand and go along with the price increase	**2**	**3** Pay the increased price but with reservations about it	**4**	**5** Strongly object and refuse to pay the increased price

C. In your contacts with your customer, how often do they bring up the subject of costs?

1 Seldom	**2**	**3** Occasionally	**4**	**5** Frequently

D. How difficult is it for your customers to pass on price increases to their customers?

1 Not a big problem	**2**	**3** Difficult but possible	**4**	**5** Very difficult if not impossible

E. What is happening with your customer's other costs other than what they pay for your product or service?

1 Not Increasing	**2**	**3** Fairly Stable	**4**	**5** Increasing

(See next page for scoring)

Exhibit 13-A
Customer Cost Calculator Scoring

Instructions: Add up the numbers of each of your answers. Find where your customer's score corresponds to one of the following profiles:

Score

5–10   Although still important, costs for your product are not a major factor for your customer

10–15   Cost are lower on your customer's priorities or concerns, but are still important

15–20   Costs could be a factor in your customer's decision to continue doing business with you

20–25   Costs are of great concern to your customer

Strategy #14

Just-in-Time Opportunities

+					
Relationship	1. Know the Customer	6. What's in a Name?	11. Understand the Customer's Needs	16. Creating Buying Habits	21. Teamwork
	2. Build Rapport	7. Selling Up, Down, All Around	12. Empowering Customers	17. Selling Service	22. Adapting to Change
	3. Honesty is the Best Policy	8. Contingency Selling	13. Cutting Costs	18. Full-Service Selling	23. Beating the Competition
	4. Understand the Customer's Perspective	9. Creating the Need	**14. Just-in-Time Opportunities**	19. Global Approach	24. Creative Selling
−	5. Selling the "Sizzle"	10. Having the Latest Technology	15. Pull-Through Sales	20. Value-Added Sales	25. Worth the Price

−   **Performance**   **+**

Sales Strategy

Relationship–lower
Performance–moderate

Just-in-time concepts have become very popular in many business applications such as inventory control and delivery. Just-in-time means that the product or even service is provided at the exact time that it is needed by the customer. In this strategy, just-in-time as it applies to selling significantly affects your relationship with the customer only if it is *not* on time. Similarly, performance really becomes important to the customer only if it is late rather than just-in-time. The concept of just-in-time sales represents unique windows of opportunity to be of greater value to the customer.

Activity

The Just-in-Time Opportunities strategy deals with the timing of making the sale to the customer. The focus of this strategy is in finding windows of opportunities to provide sales as well as service at the very moment that the customer needs it. These opportunities are referred to as windows of opportunity to sell more to the customer.

Time

40 minutes

Resources

Exhibits 14-A and 14-B

Presentation

Review where Just-in-Time Opportunities fits into the Sales Strategy Matrix and why it is positioned where it is.

Present Exhibit 14-A, Just-in-Time Sales Opportunities. Review the concept of just-in-time selling opportunities with participants. Take time to ensure that participants understand the analogy of windows of opportunities to selling to the customer as described in Exhibit 14-A.

Present Exhibit 14-B, Discovering Windows of Opportunity. Review the example of a window of opportunity presented in the exhibit. Ask participants to identify windows of opportunities in their own situations using Exhibit 14-B.

Exhibit 14-A
Just-in-Time Sales Opportunities

There are certain windows of opportunity to sell to the customer. Sometimes these windows will open for very brief periods of time, and then maybe only a crack. These windows are those unique moments in time that the customer may be most inclined or even motivated to buy. It is up to you to take advantage of these windows of opportunity before they close again or become locked shut possibly forever.

These windows of opportunity may present themselves in many different variations. Sometimes it may be up to you to not only identify these windows of opportunity, but to open them as well.

Exhibit 14-B
Discovering Windows of Opportunity

Discovering windows of opportunity to provide just-in-time selling to your customers can be very important to your success. These "windows" may be uniquely different for each customer and in each situation.

An example of such a window of opportunity might occur during a major change in the customer's business. The customer's requirements and needs may be vastly different than before perhaps in ways they never anticipated. Discovering these needs can create these new sales opportunities.

What might be some of these windows of opportunity for you to sell to your customers?

_____   _____

_____   _____

_____   _____

_____   _____

_____   _____

_____   _____

_____   _____

_____   _____

_____   _____

Strategy #15

Pull-Through Sales

+					
	1. Know the Customer	6. What's in a Name?	11. Understand the Customer's Needs	16. Creating Buying Habits	21. Teamwork
	2. Build Rapport	7. Selling Up, Down, All Around	12. Empowering Customers	17. Selling Service	22. Adapting to Change
	3. Honesty is the Best Policy	8. Contingency Selling	13. Cutting Costs	18. Full-Service Selling	23. Beating the Competition
	4. Understand the Customer's Perspective	9. Creating the Need	14. Just-in-Time Opportunities	19. Global Approach	24. Creative Selling
	5. Selling the "Sizzle"	10. Having the Latest Technology	15. **Pull-Through Sales**	20. Value-Added Sales	25. Worth the Price

Relationship (vertical axis, + to −)

Performance (horizontal axis, − to +)

Sales Strategy

Relationship—lowest
Performance—moderate

Pull-through sales is like reaching your goals through indirect methods. In other words, you achieve one thing by accomplishing something else. Although this might sound rather confusing, it is really very simple. Selling one thing puts you in a favorable position to sell a related or complementary product or service. Because pull-through sales creates the need or demand for a particular product or service, the relationship with the customer is less important. Performance is still important, but because of the unique situation pull-through sales can create for a salesperson, performance may only become a factor if it becomes a problem.

Activity

The Pull-Through Sales strategy is designed to help participants identify ways in which they might be able to generate additional sales using this concept. In this activity, participants will be asked to develop ideas of their own concerning how they can create additional pull-through sales of their own.

Time

45 minutes

Resources

Exhibits 15-A and 15-B

Presentation

Review where Pull-Through Sales fits into the Sales Strategy Matrix and why it is positioned where it is.

Spend enough time discussing the concept of pull-through sales to participants to ensure that they understand how to apply it with their own customers.

Review the various examples provided in Exhibit 15-A and apply those most appropriate for the participants. As a group, ask them to think of additional examples that would apply to their business and customers.

Using Exhibit 15-B, instruct participants to develop specific examples of pull-through opportunities that exist with their customers. In addition, they should identify why each of the opportunities would be beneficial to their customers. Point out that these benefits should and could become their major selling points to their customers for these pull-through sales.

Exhibit 15-A
Pull-Through Sales

Pull-through sales involve additional sales that a customer might want or need to purchase as a result of something he/she has already bought. In a way, these are sales that you "pull through" the original purchase made by the customer.

An important part of the service that you provide to your customers can be these pull-through sales. Pull-through sales are those things that greatly enhance the customer's satisfaction or enjoyment of their original purchase.

Examples of Pull-Through Sales

- For example, in the fast food business an example of pull-through selling might be, "Would you like fries or a drink with your sandwich?"

- In a retail environment, pull-through selling might sound like, "Would you like to look at a new pair of shoes to go with your new suit?"

- In an industrial setting, you could suggest a higher quality product to ensure that it meets the usage demands that might be experienced.

- In a service industry, additional services could be offered or for extended periods of time.

Exhibit 15-B
Pulling Through for Your Customers

What are some ways in which you could use pull-through sales with your customer(s)? Complete the pulling-through chart below to identify ways that you can actually provide benefits to the customer using this concept.

Pull-Through Opportunity	Benefits to Customer
_____	_____
_____	_____
_____	_____
_____	_____
_____	_____
_____	_____
_____	_____
_____	_____
_____	_____
_____	_____
_____	_____

Strategy #16

Creating Buying Habits

+				
1. Know the Customer	6. What's in a Name?	11. Understand the Customer's Needs	**16. Creating Buying Habits**	21. Teamwork
2. Build Rapport	7. Selling Up, Down, All Around	12. Empowering Customers	17. Selling Service	22. Adapting to Change
3. Honesty is the Best Policy	8. Contingency Selling	13. Cutting Costs	18. Full-Service Selling	23. Beating the Competition
4. Understand the Customer's Perspective	9. Creating the Need	14. Just-in-Time Opportunities	19. Global Approach	24. Creative Selling
5. Selling the "Sizzle"	10. Having the Latest Technology	15. Pull-Through Sales	20. Value-Added Sales	25. Worth the Price

Relationship (vertical axis, + to –)

Performance (horizontal axis, – to +)

Sales Strategy

Relationship—highest
Performance—higher

The positioning of this strategy on the matrix emphasizes how important relationships are to having customers continue buying from you. However, you can depend on customer loyalty to go only so far. Backing up this loyalty must be a continued history of excellent performance.

Activity

The activity focuses on how customers develop buying habits and the influence participants can have in supporting these habits.

Time

45 minutes

Resources

Exhibits 16-A, 16-B, and 16-C; flipchart

Presentation

Review where Creating Buying Habits fits into the Sales Strategy Matrix and why it is positioned where it is.

With the popularity of the book by Dr. Stephen Covey, *7 Habits of Highly Effective People,* the concept of habits is getting a great deal of attention. Begin the presentation by talking about the topic of habits. Ask participants to share their thoughts about habits and to develop a definition of the term. Write their definitions or descriptions of habits on the flipchart.

Present Exhibit 16-A, which provides a definition of the word *habit.* Compare this definition to the group's suggestions. Emphasize that there may be no absolute right or wrong definition; it is more a matter of people's perceptions about what habits may or may not be. How someone views a particular habit can have a tremendous influence on how this habit is perpetuated or maintained.

Introduce the notion that sometimes habits get a bad name. In other words, when people hear the word *habit,* they immediately think of a bad habit. But as Dr. Covey points out in his book, habits can help people become more effective.

Ask the group what habits they would want their customers to develop with regards to buying from them.

Present Exhibit 16-B, Creating New Habits. Ask participants how they develop new habits for themselves and how they feel about the concept that you need to repeat something 21 times in order for it to develop into a new habit.

Pass out copies of Exhibit 16-C, Your Customers' Buying Habits, and have participants complete it. After everyone has answered the questions in the exhibit, ask participants to share their ideas about creating customers' buying habits.

Exhibit 16-A

Definition:

> *habit:* **a routine or frequently repeated behavior or action**

Exhibit 16-B
Creating New Habits

You need to repeat something 21 times
in order for it to develop into a new habit.

Exhibit 16-C
Your Customers' Buying Habits

Answer the questions that follow concerning your customer's buying habits.

1. Do your customers buy from you on a regular basis?

   _____ Yes   _____ No

2. If "yes," is there a pattern to when they buy from you, and if so, what is this pattern?

   _____

   _____

   _____

3. What is maintaining or supporting these buying habits of your customers?

   _____

   _____

   _____

4. What can you do to prevent these buying habits from being broken?

   _____

   _____

   _____

5. If you answered "no" to question 1, what is it that keeps customers from buying from you again?

   _____

   _____

   _____

6. What can you do to change these habits of customers from not giving you repeat business to continuing to buy from you?

   _____

   _____

   _____

Strategy #17

Selling Service

+					
	1. Know the Customer	6. What's in a Name?	11. Understand the Customer's Needs	16. Creating Buying Habits	21. Teamwork
Relationship	2. Build Rapport	7. Selling Up, Down, All Around	12. Empowering Customers	**17. Selling Service**	22. Adapting to Change
	3. Honesty is the Best Policy	8. Contingency Selling	13. Cutting Costs	18. Full-Service Selling	23. Beating the Competition
	4. Understand the Customer's Perspective	9. Creating the Need	14. Just-in-Time Opportunities	19. Global Approach	24. Creative Selling
–	5. Selling the "Sizzle"	10. Having the Latest Technology	15. Pull-Through Sales	20. Value-Added Sales	25. Worth the Price
	–		**Performance**		**+**

Sales Strategy

Relationship—higher
Performance—higher

The Selling Service strategy focuses highly on both relationships and performance. Conceivably, it would be possible to provide service that would satisfy the customer with only a strong relationship or a strong performance, but it would be very difficult.

Activity

This activity focuses on the service aspect of sales. You don't necessarily have to be in the service industry to emphasize service to your customers. Everything that is sold provides a service of some kind to the customer. In fact, it is the service that is provided after the sale of a product that often becomes the most important factor in customer satisfaction.

Time

35 minutes

Resources

Exhibits 17-A and 17-B

Presentation

Review where Selling Service fits into the Sales Strategy Matrix and why it is positioned where it is.

Ask participants the first question presented in Exhibit 17-A. Lead a discussion about how participants felt when they received poor service and how likely they were to keep doing business with that supplier.

Next, ask the second question in Exhibit 17-A. Again, discuss how participants felt when they received better service than they expected.

Discuss how different these two experiences were for participants.

Ask participants the following question: "Say that the supplier in the second question did not provide quite as high a quality product as that of the supplier in the first question. Which supplier would you continue to give your business to?"

Present Exhibit 17-B, The Power of Service. Have participants answer the four questions in Part I.

After reviewing the concept of the power of service, introduce the idea of underestimating the power of service as explained in Part II of the exhibit.

There are a number of ways to determine if you are currently underestimating the power of service to your customers. One of the most efficient and practical methods would be a customer service satisfaction survey that provides a quantitative measurement similar to that in the example just provided. If you already use a customer survey of similar design, you could use it to estimate if you are currently underutilizing the power of service to your customers and by what factor.

Once you have identified that you may be underestimating the importance of service to the customer, you should begin developing strategies to improve your service to better meet the expectations and requirements of your customers.

The next activity is designed to help you identify ways to provide more complete customer service and may help you develop ways to address underestimating the power of service.

Exhibit 17-A
Service Sells

Think about an instance when you purchased a product, but didn't receive the service you needed or expected afterward. How did this make you feel as a customer? Did you continue doing business with them?

Now, think of another experience when you were pleased, even delighted, with the service you received as a result of a similar purchase as the first example. As a customer, how did this make you feel? How did you feel about continuing to do business with this supplier in this case?

How different were these two buying experiences? If everything else was equal concerning the quality of value of what you were buying, who would you prefer to give your business to?

Exhibit 17-B
The Power of Service

Part I

1. Do you think service is important to your customers?

2. Do you believe that your customers would want to have better service from you?

3. Would providing better service to your customers translate into increased sales?

4. In other words, does service really sell?

Part II

Let's assume that your answer to each of these questions was "yes" (as it probably was!). Then it is very possible that you are currently underestimating the power of service. The question is, "By what factor are you underestimating the power of service?" For example, say that your customers feel that on a scale of 1 to 10 (10 being the highest) that your service would be rated as an 8. If on this same scale you only considered service to be a 4, then you underestimated the power of service by a factor of 2.

By what factor would you estimate that you might be underestimating the power of service to your customers?

Strategy #18

Full-Service Selling

+					
	1. Know the Customer	6. What's in a Name?	11. Understand the Customer's Needs	16. Creating Buying Habits	21. Teamwork
	2. Build Rapport	7. Selling Up, Down, All Around	12. Empowering Customers	17. Selling Service	22. Adapting to Change
	3. Honesty is the Best Policy	8. Contingency Selling	13. Cutting Costs	**18. Full-Service Selling**	23. Beating the Competition
	4. Understand the Customer's Perspective	9. Creating the Need	14. Just-in-Time Opportunities	19. Global Approach	24. Creative Selling
	5. Selling the "Sizzle"	10. Having the Latest Technology	15. Pull-Through Sales	20. Value-Added Sales	25. Worth the Price

Relationship (left vertical axis, from − to +)

−   **Performance**   +

Sales Strategy

Relationship—moderate
Performance—higher

Providing full-service selling is becoming more of a necessity than a luxury in business today. *Full service* means that you do as much for your customers as you possibly can. Customers are busy running their own business and often value having someone who can take over certain aspects of their responsibilities. Relationships under these circumstances are less important than actual performance. The more customers learn to depend on you, the less direction they need to give you. In this case—no news can be good news.

Activity

This activity asks participants to think about ways in which they can provide a greater level of service to their customers. Participants are challenged to fully explore the idea of what providing full service really can mean to the customer and what needs to be done in order to reach this level of service.

Time

30 minutes

Resources

Exhibits 18-A, 18-B, and 18-C

Presentation

Review where Full-Service Selling fits into the Sales Strategy Matrix and why it is positioned where it is.

Ask participants to think of providing customer service as a "glass" to be filled.

Present Exhibit 18-A, and ask participants if they presently view the level of service they provide their customers as being half empty or half full. In other words, do they see greater opportunities to fill the "glass" or is it already full enough?

Provide a copy of Exhibit 18-B for each participant. Read the instructions at the top of the exhibit and have participants identify the increment measurements on the side of the glass for their own situations. If some participants have difficulty understanding how to complete this exercise, provide examples of what might be written in the increment measurements, such as replenishing customer inventories, completing governmental forms, providing upgrades, etc.

Present Exhibit 18-C, which challenges participants to develop ideas about how they can move toward providing full service to their customers. Distribute a copy of Exhibit 18-C to each person to develop their own strategies.

After everyone has completed 18-C, discuss as a group some of the strategies that participants developed and how they could be implemented.

Exhibit 18-A

Is your customer service "glass" half empty or half full?

Exhibit 18-B
Reaching Full Service

Just for a moment, think of providing full service to your customer as if it were a drinking glass to be filled. Written on the side of the glass are measurements of the amount of service you can potentially provide the customer.

Reaching full customer service is already marked at the top of the glass. Identify how you would describe the other increments in terms of the level of service that you could provide your customers.

Full Customer Service

Exhibit 18-C

How can you "fill" your customer service "glass"?

_____

_____

_____

_____

_____

_____

_____

_____

_____

_____

Strategy #19

Global Approach

+					
	1. Know the Customer	6. What's in a Name?	11. Understand the Customer's Needs	16. Creating Buying Habits	21. Teamwork
	2. Build Rapport	7. Selling Up, Down, All Around	12. Empowering Customers	17. Selling Service	22. Adapting to Change
Relationship	3. Honesty is the Best Policy	8. Contingency Selling	13. Cutting Costs	18. Full-Service Selling	23. Beating the Competition
	4. Understand the Customer's Perspective	9. Creating the Need	14. Just-in-Time Opportunities	**19. Global Approach**	24. Creative Selling
	5. Selling the "Sizzle"	10. Having the Latest Technology	15. Pull-Through Sales	20. Value-Added Sales	25. Worth the Price

–   **Performance**   +

Sales Strategy

Relationship—lower
Performance—higher

Relationships get more complex the more global they become. Being able to continuously and consistently provide the quality customers require on a large or global scale can be a tremendous challenge. The concept of global doesn't necessarily have to refer to international business. Global may also relate to dealing with the customer's entire organization, regardless of how many international borders this may cross.

Activity

This activity is designed to help participants think more globally in their sales strategies. For the purposes of this activity, the term *global* doesn't necessarily have to refer to international borders. Rather, thinking globally in this case could refer to the customer's entire organization and operations.

Time

40 minutes

Resources

Exhibits 19-A and 19-B; literature including annual reports about participants' customers; flipchart

Presentation

Review where Global Approach fits into the Sales Strategy Matrix and why it is positioned where it is.

Ask participants what they think of when they hear the term *global* as it relates to customers. You should expect to hear responses that refer to doing business with customers around the world. Ask the group what opportunities and challenges a global sales strategy might create. List these responses on a flipchart.

Next introduce the concept that global does not necessarily mean across international borders and refer to Exhibit 19-A, Going Global. *Global* in this sense relates to the customer's entire organization and operations. Now ask participants what comes to mind when they think of *global* in this sense. Write their responses on another sheet of flipchart paper and tape it to the wall next to the other sheet. Compare the similarities between these two lists. Look for commonalities that might be included on these two lists, such as different goals, ways of doing business, even cultural or language (terminology, technical descriptions, etc.) differences.

Distribute a copy of Exhibit 19-B, Global Opportunities, to each participant. Have participants answer the questions on the exhibit.

The focus of this activity should be on completing the last question on Exhibit 19-B, which asks participants to develop a strategy for approaching their customers to ask them for more global opportunities to be of service to them.

Exhibit 19-A
Going Global

Going global may sound like an awesome challenge. After all, the world is a very big place. However, a global sales strategy can be not only manageable, but also can be a much more efficient way of doing business with your customers. *Global* can mean many things in addition to international dealings. *Global* can mean being totally inclusive, serving the customer's entire organization.

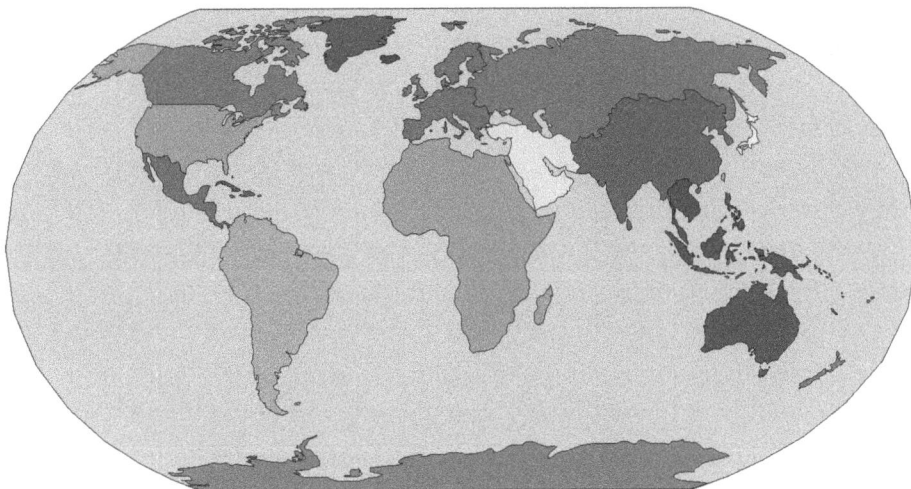

Exhibit 19-B
Global Opportunities

Answer the following questions to gain a better understanding of how a global sales strategy could help you better serve your customers.

Are there additional opportunities for you to sell your products/service to your customers?

_____

_____

What would be some of these opportunities?

_____

_____

_____

_____

_____

How could providing this more global approach to your customers enable you to better serve their needs?

_____

_____

_____

_____

_____

How could you make your customers more aware of these benefits of going global and gain additional business?

_____

_____

_____

_____

_____

Strategy #20

Value-Added Sales

+					
	1. Know the Customer	6. What's in a Name?	11. Understand the Customer's Needs	16. Creating Buying Habits	21. Teamwork
	2. Build Rapport	7. Selling Up, Down, All Around	12. Empowering Customers	17. Selling Service	22. Adapting to Change
	3. Honesty is the Best Policy	8. Contingency Selling	13. Cutting Costs	18. Full-Service Selling	23. Beating the Competition
	4. Understand the Customer's Perspective	9. Creating the Need	14. Just-in-Time Opportunities	19. Global Approach	24. Creative Selling
	5. Selling the "Sizzle"	10. Having the Latest Technology	15. Pull-Through Sales	**20. Value-Added Sales**	25. Worth the Price

Relationship (vertical axis, + top, – bottom)

Performance (horizontal axis, – left, + right)

Sales Strategy

Relationship—lowest
Performance—higher

The term *value-added* speaks almost entirely about performance. *Value* in this case can supersede relationships. Even the strongest customer relationship can be replaced by a value-added sales strategy. Value is the bottomline to customers, and your ability to perform to meet this critical requirement can determine if you keep or gain their business or not.

Activity

The objective of this activity is to help participants identify when and how to focus on value when dealing with their customers. The activity draws the distinction between added costs to the customer as opposed to added value. This activity can also be useful in helping participants find new customers, particularly when they can identify those circumstances when competitors are using a high relationship-focused sales strategy rather than a high performance-focused sales strategy.

Time

40 minutes

Resources

Exhibits 20-A, 20-B, 20-C, and 20-D; flipchart

Presentation

Review where Value-Added Sales fits into the Sales Strategy Matrix and why it is positioned where it is.

Begin the activity by asking participants what they look for when they purchase a product or service. Write their responses on a flipchart. It is very likely that the word *value* will appear on this list. If not, there will be other similar terms that mean essentially the same thing. Highlight, by underlining or circling, these value-related terms suggested by the group, and again emphasize how important value is to any customer.

Present Exhibit 20-A, Cost Versus Value. Ask the group what they perceive the difference to be between the two, particularly from their perspective as a customer.

Next present Exhibit 20-B, which shows the distinction between *cost* and *value.* As explained in this exhibit, *costs* are merely expenditures without potential for return or gain. *Value* results from something that gives you a return or gain on your investment. Ask participants how they would want their customers to view paying for the product or service they provide.

Review Exhibit 20-C, Added Value (+V) Estimator, with participants. Have them complete the questions and added-value calculations.

Using Exhibit 20-D, help participants develop their own strategies on how to communicate to a customer that their product/service can add value to the customer's business.

Conclude the activity by asking participants how they could use their value-added strategy to gain new customers, particularly those who might be doing business with a supplier focused more on the relationship factor than performance.

Exhibit 20-A
Cost Versus Value

**What is the distinction to a customer between
cost and added value when buying a product or service?**

Exhibit 20-B

Definitions:

costs: expenditures with no potential for gain or return

added value: expenditures that provide a gain or return on the investment of resources

Exhibit 20-C
Added Value (+V) Estimator

Answer the following to determine ways in which your product/service can become added value (+V) opportunities to your customers.

Step 1: How does your product/service currently improve your customer's overall performance?

Step 2: What would be your estimate of the return on the investment (expressed as a percentage of the amount spent) your customer spends on your product/service?

Step 3: How could you help your customer realize greater returns on their investment in your product or service?

Step 4: What would be the potential gains to the customer as a result of the additional added value?

Step 5: Considering all of the previous four added-value steps, what potentially would be the estimated +V to your customers in terms of such benefits as increased market share, lower costs, greater customer satisfaction, stronger customer loyalty, etc.?

Exhibit 20-D
Developing an
Added-Value Strategy

Using the concepts and tools presented in this activity, develop a strategy for better communication with your customer about how your product/service can add value to their business.

_____

_____

_____

_____

_____

_____

_____

_____

_____

_____

_____

_____

Strategy #21

Teamwork

+					
	1. Know the Customer	6. What's in a Name?	11. Understand the Customer's Needs	16. Creating Buying Habits	**21. Teamwork**
	2. Build Rapport	7. Selling Up, Down, All Around	12. Empowering Customers	17. Selling Service	22. Adapting to Change
Relationship	3. Honesty is the Best Policy	8. Contingency Selling	13. Cutting Costs	18. Full-Service Selling	23. Beating the Competition
	4. Understand the Customer's Perspective	9. Creating the Need	14. Just-in-Time Opportunities	19. Global Approach	24. Creative Selling
	5. Selling the "Sizzle"	10. Having the Latest Technology	15. Pull-Through Sales	20. Value-Added Sales	25. Worth the Price

− **Performance** +

Sales Strategy

Relationship—highest
Performance—highest

Developing a teamwork sales strategy with your customer requires both a strong relationship to be established plus a proven performance record. Within an organization, employees are usually assigned to be part of a team. On the other hand, customers decide which suppliers will be part of their team. Customers will be highly selective concerning who they want on their team. Striving to achieve this status requires a total commitment to build both the relationship and performance history necessary to establish the customer's trust in you to be considered part of their team.

Activity

Teamwork and teambuilding are receiving a great deal of attention today and for good reason. By working together with the customer as a team, you create synergy. Synergy is best defined as the "whole being greater than the sum of the parts—2 + 2 equals a number much greater than 4." Synergy allows each team member to reach their fullest potential both individually and as a team. This creates a win-win situation for everyone. This activity includes a series of four scenarios designed to help participants better understand and appreciate how to synergize with the customer and create a working relationship based on teamwork. In each scenario, both the customer's perspective and the participant's perspective as the supplier are presented. The objective in each of these exercises is to develop a Teamwork strategy that would be a win-win for both the customer and the participant as the supplier.

Time

45 minutes

Resources

A copy of Exhibits 21-A, 21-B, 21-C, and 21-D for each participant

Presentation

Review where Teamwork fits into the Sales Strategy Matrix and why it is positioned where it is.

In Exhibits 21-A, 21-B, 21-C, and 21-D, there are four different scenarios, each describing how both the customer and the supplier might perceive a situation relating to their business relationship together. Each of these descriptions represents what would be a "win" for either the customer or the supplier (participants), or how achieving this "win" could possibly create a "lose" for the other party.

Depending on group size, break participants into groups of 3 to 5 people. Assign one of the four scenarios to each group.

Instruct each group to read both the customer's perspective and the supplier's perspective. Each group should develop a Teamwork strategy for their assigned scenario that creates a win-win for everyone.

As an alternative, you could break participants into two-person teams and assign the customer role and supplier role to each. Then together they should develop a Teamwork strategy for the situation. After everyone has completed their scenarios, reconvene the group and ask for a summary of each team's problem and the Teamwork strategies they developed.

Exhibit 21-A
Scenario 1: The Right Price

Instructions: Read each of the following sales situations describing the perspective of the customer as well as your perspective (the supplier's). Then come up with a Teamwork strategy that would be a win-win scenario for both of you.

Customer's Perspective: The customer is very concerned with costs and has been putting a great deal of pressure on the supplier to maintain or even lower prices. The customer has even hinted that if the supplier doesn't comply with their pricing requests, they will take their business elsewhere.

Your Perspective: You are already operating at a very small profit margin due to the extremely competitive nature of your business. The customer's demands could force you into a financial loss position if you continued selling to them under these circumstances.

Teamwork Strategy:

_____

_____

_____

_____

_____

_____

Exhibit 21-B
Scenario 2: Quality Standards

Instructions: Read each of the following sales situations describing the perspective of the customer as well as your perspective (the supplier's). Then come up with a Teamwork strategy that would be a win-win scenario for both of you.

Customer's Perspective: The customer keeps demanding stricter and stricter quality standards from you as part of their ISO 9000 certification process.

Your Perspective: Although you fully understand why the customer is requesting better quality performance from you, achieving these higher standards has presented many very challenging problems for your company, including increased costs.

Teamwork Strategy:

_____

_____

_____

_____

_____

_____

Exhibit 21-C
Scenario 3: Competition versus Sole Supplier

Instructions: Read each of the following sales situations describing the perspective of the customer as well as your perspective (the supplier's). Then come up with a Teamwork strategy that would be a win-win scenario for both of you.

Customer's Perspective: The customer likes to have a number of different suppliers to ensure uninterrupted supply and service at all times and regardless of the situation. They also believe that this creates a healthy competition among their suppliers as each one strives to keep their share of the business.

Your Perspective: You believe that if you were exclusively given all of this customer's business, you could provide them better quality and more competitive pricing than they are presently receiving from you with multiple suppliers.

Teamwork Strategy:

_____

_____

_____

_____

_____

_____

_____

Exhibit 21-D
Scenario 4: Warranties

Instructions: Read each of the following sales situations describing the perspective of the customer as well as your perspective (the supplier's). Then come up with a Teamwork strategy that would be a win-win scenario for both of you.

Customer's Perspective: The customer would like to have a longer warranty on your product/service. They claim that they have already talked to your major competitors who are willing to provide these warranties.

Your Perspective: Your legal, technical, and financial advisors have all advised you that extending these warranties would not be a good business decision and question how any of your competitors could profitably do this.

Teamwork Strategy:

_____

_____

_____

_____

_____

_____

Strategy #22

Adapting to Change

+					
	1. Know the Customer	6. What's in a Name?	11. Understand the Customer's Needs	16. Creating Buying Habits	21. Teamwork
	2. Build Rapport	7. Selling Up, Down, All Around	12. Empowering Customers	17. Selling Service	**22. Adapting to Change**
Relationship	3. Honesty is the Best Policy	8. Contingency Selling	13. Cutting Costs	18. Full-Service Selling	23. Beating the Competition
	4. Understand the Customer's Perspective	9. Creating the Need	14. Just-in-Time Opportunities	19. Global Approach	24. Creative Selling
	5. Selling the "Sizzle"	10. Having the Latest Technology	15. Pull-Through Sales	20. Value-Added Sales	25. Worth the Price

−   **Performance**   **+**

Sales Strategy

Relationship—higher
Performance—highest

Change can be difficult—even a traumatic experience for customers. Helping your customers adapt to change requires you to provide reassurance that they will still receive the same quality service or product as they did before the change. Your relationship with the customer can become very important as you help them through these transitions. Even more important to the customer is the ultimate result of the change. If the customer is not happy afterward, all the reassurance in the world will not make up for what the customer perceives they have lost. However, the key word is *perceives*. How you present the change can have a great deal to do with how it is accepted by the customer.

Activity

This activity provides participants with advice about how to help customers accept the inevitable changes that occur as they do business together. So much of how well the customer accepts change is dependent on how it is perceived by the customer. There are a number of strategies and approaches presented to help customers move through these transitions more smoothly and with the least disruption to their business.

Time

45 minutes

Resources

Exhibits 22-A and 22-B

Presentation

Review where Adapting to Change fits into the Sales Strategy Matrix and why it is positioned where it is.

Present Exhibit 22-A, Stages of Customer Acceptance to Change. This model shows the four stages that customers will often go through as you introduce change to them. The model illustrates that these stages are typically in a progression, meaning that customers experience each in the sequence shown: (1) resistance, (2) seeking alternatives, (3) adapting, and (4) acceptance. The directional arrows shown in the model indicate the direction of this progression as well as how these changes might be affecting the attitude of your customer during the transition. Understanding how the customer might be feeling during these various stages of the change process can be very important to helping the customer move through these stages.

Review and introduce Exhibit 22-B, Tips on Helping the Customer Adapt to Change. Emphasize the following points:

1. Complexity. Don't underestimate the complexity of change. Whenever introducing change, there is often a tendency to simplify or fail to anticipate problems and complexities involved. Take the time and effort to gain a better understanding of what the effects of the change will have on the customer. The better you can demonstrate this understanding to the customer, the more confident and accepting of the change the customer will be.

2. Communications. Communicate as much information to the customer as possible. The rule here should be to over-communicate rather than not share enough information. Timeliness of your communications will also become critical. Hearing "yesterday's news" will not help the customer adapt to the changes being made today.

3. Time. Allow the customer enough time to get used to and adapt to the changes in stages or phases rather than all at once. Again, allow enough time between each stage for the customer to understand and respond appropriately to the change before moving on to the next change.

4. Support. It is essential that the customer feels that they have your support during this period of change. This support could come in many ways: providing technical assistance, training or education, or even moral support and reassurance to the customer.

5. Patience. Above all, you might need to be patient with the customer as they adapt to the change. Remember how difficult change can be for people.

Conclude the activity by asking participants the following question:

"What do you think the pace of change will be like in the future with regards to doing business with your customers?"

The answer that you will most likely receive is that this pace will accelerate in the future. The point is that the ability to adapt to change will become an even more important skill for everyone to develop as we move ahead in today's fast-paced world.

Exhibit 22-A
Stages of
Customer Acceptance to Change

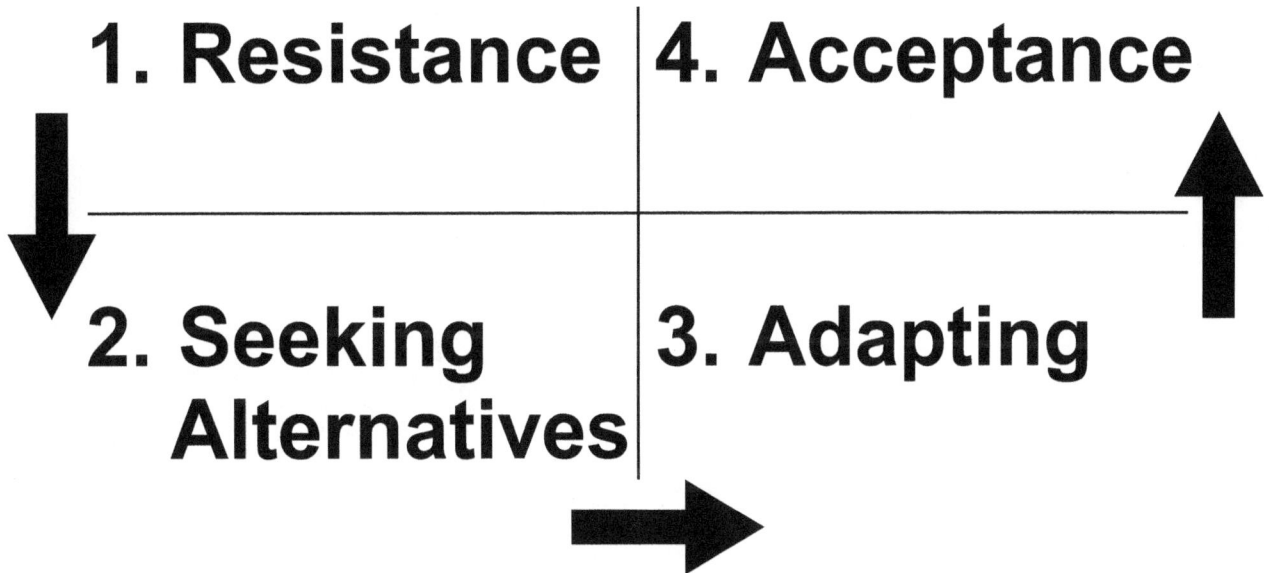

1. Resistance	4. Acceptance
2. Seeking Alternatives	3. Adapting

Exhibit 22-B
Tips on Helping the
Customer Adapt to Change

1. Don't underestimate the complexity of change.

2. Communicate as much information to the customer as possible.

3. Allow the customer enough time to get used to and deal with the changes you are introducing.

4. Provide the customer with the support they need during the change process.

5. Be patient with the customer during the change process.

Strategy #23

Beating the Competition

+				
1. Know the Customer	6. What's in a Name?	11. Understand the Customer's Needs	16. Creating Buying Habits	21. Teamwork
2. Build Rapport	7. Selling Up, Down, All Around	12. Empowering Customers	17. Selling Service	22. Adapting to Change
3. Honesty is the Best Policy	8. Contingency Selling	13. Cutting Costs	18. Full-Service Selling	**23. Beating the Competition**
4. Understand the Customer's Perspective	9. Creating the Need	14. Just-in-Time Opportunities	19. Global Approach	24. Creative Selling
5. Selling the "Sizzle"	10. Having the Latest Technology	15. Pull-Through Sales	20. Value-Added Sales	25. Worth the Price

Relationship (vertical axis, + top, – bottom)

−   **Performance**   +

Sales Strategy

Relationship—moderate
Performance—highest

You have to be really good to beat the competition. This requires you to not only be able to outperform your competition, but also to convince the customer that you can. This challenge becomes tougher and tougher as the competition for customers increases. This strategy forces you to continuously find ways to improve your performance to ensure that you stay ahead of the competition.

Activity

Beating the competition can apply to sales strategies focused on maintaining existing customers as well as finding new customers. The activity involves a case entitled "Who Gets the Business?" that participants read and then discuss.

Time

45 minutes

Resources

Exhibits 23-A, 23-B, and 23-C

Presentation

Review where Beating the Competition fits into the Sales Strategy Matrix and why it is positioned where it is.

Introduce this activity as one that focuses on both keeping the competition from taking away the customers you already have as well as finding new customers.

Ask participants to read the case study found in Exhibit 23-A, entitled Who Gets the Business? Allow them at least 10 to 15 minutes to thoroughly understand the situation presented in the case study.

After everyone has had the opportunity to finish reading the case study, present Exhibit 23-B, The Sales Call, and ask participants to answer individually the question, "What will you say to the purchasing manager to get Tough Customer's business and beat your competition?"

After everyone has answered the question, ask the group to share their answers. Exhibit 23-C includes a list of points that should be made during the appointment with Tough Customer's purchasing manager, described in Exhibit 23-B. As an alternative, you could conduct a role play in which you assume the part of the purchasing manager. Have volunteers make their presentation to you in front of the other participants and allow the group to determine who gets the business.

Conclude the activity by asking participants to think about how their own current and potential relationships with customers might relate to those presented in this case study.

Exhibit 23-A
Case Study

Who Gets the Business?

This is a story about the Tough Customer Company. True to their name, they are truly a very tough customer not only to get their business, but also to keep it. Despite their reputation, they are the most sought-after account any salesperson could ever hope to "land."

The Tough Customer Company has very strict requirements that must be met in order to do business with them. These requirements go beyond just meeting product/service specifications. There is also a supplier relationship factor that fits into their buying decision-making process. Although this is believed to be a very critical part of their supplier selection decision-making process, it is also somewhat unclear what it is that they really expect or hope from suppliers in their working relationships. There have been rumors that one of their suppliers lost their business because they tried too hard to maintain a good working relationship with them. Other reports seem to indicate that others have lost favor by not trying hard enough. How to get and keep Tough Customer's business continues to be one of the greatest mysteries in the industry.

If you would ask Tough Customer how to get their business, they would tell you that it is very simple—"to be the best." Unfortunately, it will be up to you to find out what this really means to Tough Customer. In reality, they do have a few very specific requirements that must be met, which are as follows:

- All business with Tough Customer must be completed on schedule. Any delays in delivery on the part of a supplier will result in financial penalties or loss of their business.

- Tough Customer reserves the right to change specifications at any time. The only limitation they will agree to is that these changes must be reasonable and realistically obtainable by their suppliers. Unfortunately, Tough Customer also reserves the right to determine what is reasonable and realistic; however, reportedly they have basically followed what the industry standards have been in these determinations of realistic and reasonable.

- Tough Customer reserves the right to terminate doing business with a supplier at any time based on their performance. Suppliers do have this same ability to cancel their contract before it expires; however, no supplier has ever done this to date.

(continued)

Exhibit 23-A
Case Study
(concluded)

- Tough Customer has a history of asking for price reductions from its suppliers whenever their business fails to meet their expected goals.

- Tough Customer is constantly looking for the newest methods and technology to give them an advantage in the marketplace. They look for suppliers who can bring the latest and most innovative ideas to them.

- Suppliers must agree in writing to all of these conditions before doing business with Tough Customer.

Exhibit 23-B
The Sales Call

You have an appointment next week with the purchasing manager at Tough Customer. You have heard that several of your biggest competitors will also be making presentations next week.

What will you say to the purchasing manager to get Tough Customer's business and beat your competition?

Exhibit 23-C
Tough Customer Sales Call Debrief

The following are some of the points that should be made during the presentation to Tough Customer's purchasing manager:

- It is important to avoid over-promising to a potential customer, particularly one like Tough Customer.

- Ensure that you fully understand your organization's ability to meet Tough Customer's demanding schedule. You should be able to demonstrate what capabilities your company has to meet these schedule demands or what commitments you are willing to make in order to be able to.

- You should be prepared to explain how your company can and will respond to changes in specifications. You must emphasize that your organization will do whatever it realistically can do to respond to these changes. Again, be realistic in your promises. If you can't do something that is unrealistic, explain this to Tough Customer. It is likely that if you can't meet this demand, other suppliers won't be able to either.

- Explain how your company has met demanding requirements of other customers and that you intend to keep Tough Customer's business. Emphasize that if you can't keep their business, it is likely that no one else can (provided that this statement is true).

- Stand your ground on the issue of price reductions, but be willing to discuss this issue. Explain that you need to make a reasonable profit in order to stay in business yourselves during tough times. However, you need to make sure that Tough Company continues to believe that you are worth the price (see Activity 25).

- Explain your company's commitment to innovation and research to find new products/ services and that your future also depends on these new products.

- Emphasize that you view your working relationship with Tough Customer as a partnership and that you are committed to meeting their requirements, and that doing so will be mutually beneficial to both of you.

Strategy #24

Creative Selling

+					
	1. Know the Customer	6. What's in a Name?	11. Understand the Customer's Needs	16. Creating Buying Habits	21. Teamwork
	2. Build Rapport	7. Selling Up, Down, All Around	12. Empowering Customers	17. Selling Service	22. Adapting to Change
Relationship	3. Honesty is the Best Policy	8. Contingency Selling	13. Cutting Costs	18. Full-Service Selling	23. Beating the Competition
	4. Understand the Customer's Perspective	9. Creating the Need	14. Just-in-Time Opportunities	19. Global Approach	**24. Creative Selling**
_	5. Selling the "Sizzle"	10. Having the Latest Technology	15. Pull-Through Sales	20. Value-Added Sales	25. Worth the Price

—   **Performance**   +

Sales Strategy

Relationship—lower
Performance—highest

Being creative in your approach to customers is all about finding different and unique ways to educate them about the performance of your product or service. As always, relationships are still important, but the focus here is clearly on what your product/service can do for the customer.

Activity

There is a great deal of competition for customers today, and creative selling techniques can help you get their attention and stand out in the crowd. This activity challenges participants to think of and find ways to develop more creative selling strategies.

Time

35 minutes

Resources

Exhibits 24-A, 24-B, 24-C, and 24-D

Presentation

Review where Creative Selling fits into the Sales Strategy Matrix and why it is positioned where it is.

Review Exhibit 24-A, What is Creative Selling? and Exhibit 24-B, Creative Selling Technique Ideas.

Next present Exhibit 24-C, Creative Selling Techniques. This asks participants to think of ways in which they have seen creative selling techniques used most effectively and why these were so effective.

Conclude the activity with Exhibit 24-D, Creative Selling Strategies for Your Customers, which encourages participants to develop more creative selling techniques with their customers.

Remind participants that sales strategies such as creative selling might not always be appropriate or received positively by all customers or in every situation. Good judgment is necessary to evaluate when and where creative selling would be most effective. These risks need to be considered in relation to the potential benefits of a creative selling approach in each sales situation.

Exhibit 24-A
What is Creative Selling?

Creative selling techniques are designed to get the customer's attention. Creative selling helps you stand out in the crowd from the other suppliers who are also trying to get the customer's business. Creative selling might be best described as "selling outside the box" or, in other words, not being constrained by conventional or expected selling strategies typically used in your business or industry.

Creative selling is limited only by your imagination. Of course, good judgment must be exercised concerning the perceived appropriateness and receptivity of the customer of your creative selling.

Exhibit 24-B
Creative Selling Technique Ideas

Creative selling might include any number of approaches and ideas. The following are just a few ideas to get you thinking more creatively about selling:

- Humorous sales presentations

- Free introductory offers

- Competitor comparisons

- Product endorsements

- Unique facts about product/service

- Reverse psychology sales (pretending to talk the customer out of buying from you)

- Contests

- Creating a publicity event

- Parties/celebrations

- Making different contacts in the customer's organization

Exhibit 24-C
Creative Selling Techniques

What are some examples of creative selling techniques that you have seen used effectively and why?

Creative Selling Techniques	Why Effective
_____	_____
_____	_____
_____	_____
_____	_____
_____	_____
_____	_____
_____	_____
_____	_____
_____	_____
_____	_____
_____	_____
_____	_____
_____	_____

Exhibit 24-D
Creative Selling Strategies
for Your Customers

Just like the popular cliché about "thinking outside the box," creating creative selling strategies requires you to think differently about selling.

What are some creative selling strategies that you could use with your customers?

_____

_____

_____

_____

_____

_____

_____

_____

_____

_____

_____

_____

_____

_____

Strategy #25

Worth the Price

+					
	1. Know the Customer	6. What's in a Name?	11. Understand the Customer's Needs	16. Creating Buying Habits	21. Teamwork
	2. Build Rapport	7. Selling Up, Down, All Around	12. Empowering Customers	17. Selling Service	22. Adapting to Change
Relationship	3. Honesty is the Best Policy	8. Contingency Selling	13. Cutting Costs	18. Full-Service Selling	23. Beating the Competition
	4. Understand the Customer's Perspective	9. Creating the Need	14. Just-in-Time Opportunities	19. Global Approach	24. Creative Selling
I	5. Selling the "Sizzle"	10. Having the Latest Technology	15. Pull-Through Sales	20. Value-Added Sales	**25. Worth the Price**

–   **Performance**   **+**

Sales Strategy

Relationship—lowest
Performance—highest

It only makes sense that this strategy would be all performance oriented. It the customer is going to pay more money for something, then he/she has every right to expect it to be "worth the price." If not, all the relationship building that you could ever try to achieve most likely will be all for naught. This is the strategy of *doing what you said you would do and delivering on the goods.*

Activity

Worth the Price examines what might be some of the expectations that a customer would have when paying a premium price or really any price. It challenges participants to ensure their product/service is in fact worth the price.

Time

30 minutes

Resources

Exhibits 25-A and 25-B

Presentation

Review where Worth the Price fits into the Sales Strategy Matrix and why it is positioned where it is.

Introduce the activity by explaining that the focus of Worth the Price is from the customer's perspective. In other words, the true measure of the worth of your product/service is ultimately determined by the customer and communicated by their buying habits. It can be easy to fall into the deceptive trap of evaluating if your product/service is worth the price from your own perspective rather than the customer's.

Present Exhibit 25-A, Worth the Price Questionnaire, to participants. Instruct participants to answer those questions in the questionnaire that are applicable to them. Based on their individual responses, ask participants what plans and actions they might take concerning pricing issues with their customers that might be important to the customer's perceptions concerning this issue of price.

Have participants complete the first item of Exhibit 25-B, listing all the reasons they can think of concerning why their product/service is worth the price. Next, for the second item, have participants develop a strategy concerning how to ensure that their customers understand these reasons they identified.

Conclude the activity with a discussion about the importance of price to the customers and the need to remain aware of what their customer's feelings and perceptions might be about the price they are paying. Discuss how price is obviously important to the participants as suppliers to the customer: It determines the amount of revenue and ultimately profits that their company receives. There must be a balance between the pricing needs of the customer and the supplier (participants) in order for a mutually beneficial business relationship to exist.

Exhibit 25-A
Worth the Price Questionnaire

What are some ways in which your customers would determine if your service/product is "worth the price"?

_____

_____

_____

_____

Are these the same measures you would use and in what ways?

_____

_____

_____

_____

What makes your product/service worth more than what you competitors might offer at a lower price?

_____

_____

_____

_____

How can you ensure that your customers understand why your product/service is worth the price?

_____

_____

_____

_____

(continued)

Exhibit 25-A
Worth the Price Questionnaire
(continued)

What would happen if you raised your price? Would your customers still buy from you? Why?

_____

_____

_____

_____

Is there any reason to think that your customers might take their business elsewhere because of price? If so, why?

_____

_____

_____

_____

How much influence or control do you have over pricing in your organization?

_____

_____

_____

_____

Who should you tell in your organization about any pricing issues that you are aware of concerning customers?

_____

_____

_____

_____

(continued)

Exhibit 25-A: Worth the Price Questionnaire

Exhibit 25-A
Worth the Price Questionnaire
(continued)

Do your customers frequently bring up the issue of pricing with you?

_____

_____

_____

_____

When is the last time you reviewed your pricing strategy within your organization?

_____

_____

_____

_____

Where is your pricing in relation to your industry's standards?

_____

_____

_____

_____

Do you have any plans to change your pricing?

_____

_____

_____

_____

(continued)

Exhibit 25-A
Worth the Price Questionnaire
(concluded)

If so, have you communicated these plans to your customers?

_____

_____

_____

_____

What was their reaction?

_____

_____

_____

_____

Did this reaction cause you to re-think or change your pricing plans? Why or why not?

_____

_____

_____

_____

Exhibit 25-B
Communicating Worth the Price to the Customer

List as many of the reasons you can think of why your product or service is worth the price or even more to the customer:

_____

_____

_____

_____

_____

_____

Develop a strategy below to ensure that the customer is aware of these reasons and understands why your product or service is worth the price, using the reasons you listed above.

_____

_____

_____

_____

_____

_____

www.ingramcontent.com/pod-product-compliance
Lightning Source LLC
Chambersburg PA
CBHW080552220326
41599CB00032B/6447